WHATS IN A NAME.....

Some Newcastle Street names explained

Published by
Newcastle upon Tyne City Libraries & Arts

Front cover: Side, from a drawing by William Heath c1820, engraved c1880.

The maps are reproduced from Thomas Oliver's map of 1830, which also shows projected improvements to the town.

Text and photographs compiled by Anna Flowers and Maria Hoy.

ISBN 1 85795 015 1

British Library Cataloguing-in-Publication Data.
A catalogue record for this book is available from the British Library.

INTRODUCTION

Newcastle has a long and proud history. There has been a settlement here since the Romans established a military station and bridged the river in approximately A.D. 122. In 1080 a motte and bailey castle was erected by Robert Curthose, son of William the Conqueror, which gave the name Newcastle to the town. In 1177 the wooden castle was replaced by a stone building, parts of which still stand today.

Since then the town has continued to grow in importance, and became a city in 1882. The long and varied history of Newcastle is reflected in some of the street names used in the city. An indication of the Saxon inheritance is heard in the name 'chare' given to narrow lanes in this part of the world, and the physical characteristics of the old river port, its steep banks once cut by streams, are recalled in names such as Dean Street or Sandhill. The importance of the Town Walls and Towers, once described as surpassing many others 'in their strength and magnificence' (John Leland), can be noted in the many references to them in street names such as Westgate Road, Newgate Street or Tower Street. The Walls and Towers were mostly demolished during the eighteenth and nineteenth centuries as the town expanded. Famous local families, for example Percy and Neville are remembered alongside individuals like Richard Grainger and Thomas Bewick. The origins of areas such as Gallowgate and Castle Garth are recalled through the continued use of their names.

Street signs were first used in Newcastle in 1783. Since then many people have been fascinated by the origin of some of the names. The selection of photographs in this book provides some interesting snippets of information and an insight into some aspects of the history of Newcastle.

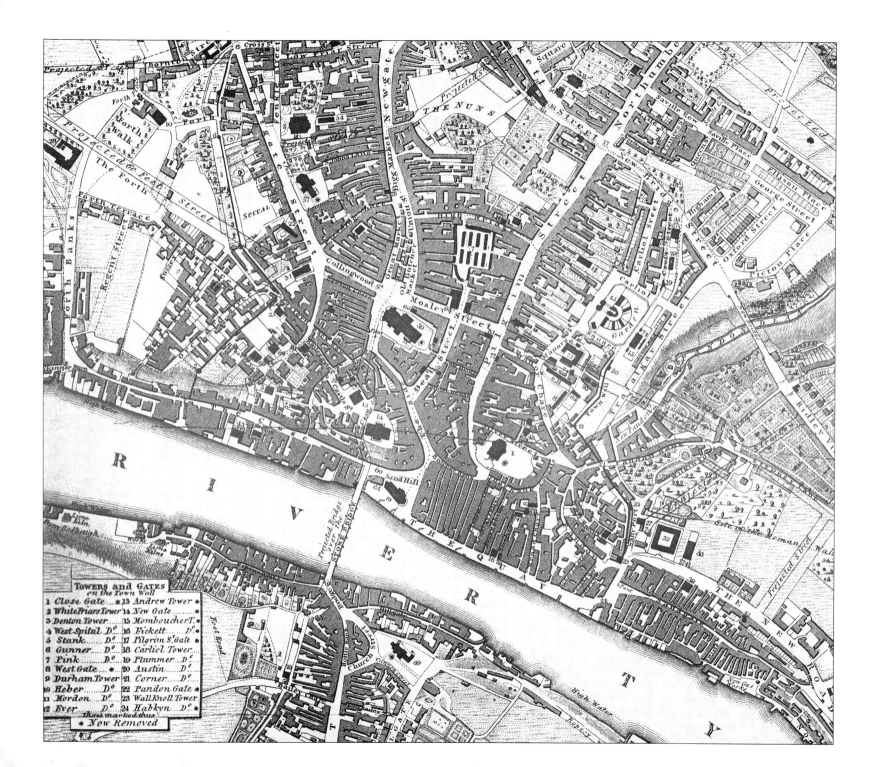

TOWERS and GATES
on the Town Wall

1 Close Gate ✱	13 Andrew Tower ✱
2 WhiteFriars Tower ✱	14 New Gate .... ✱
3 Denton Tower	15 Momboucher T.
4 West Spital D.º	16 Fickett ...... D.º
5 Stank ...... D.º	17 Pilgrim S.t Gate ✱
6 Gunner ... D.º	18 Carliel Tower ....
7 Pink ..... D.º	19 Plummer D.º
8 West Gate .... ✱	20 Austin .... D.º
9 Durham Tower	21 Corner ... D.º
10 Heber .... D.º	22 Pandon Gate ✱
11 Mordon ... D.º	23 Wall Knoll Tower ✱
12 Ever ...... D.º	24 Habkyn .. D.º ✱

those marked thus
✱ *Now Removed*

Broad Chare 1895

'Chare' is a local word for a narrow lane thought to derive from the Saxon word 'cer' or 'cerre' meaning a turning. There were once many of these narrow streets running back from the Quayside with such strange names as Blue Anchor Chare, Dark Chare, Peppercorn Chare, mostly destroyed in the disastrous fire of 1854. Broad Chare survived; its name referring to the fact that it was wide enough for a cart to pass through.

Trinity House, which is on the right hand side of Broad Chare when looking towards the river, was opened in 1492 as a meeting place for the guild of pilots and mariners, and is still in use today. This photograph was taken from the Quayside in 1895 and shows Broad Chare and Spicer Lane. The new Quayside Law Courts stand on the site of Spicer Lane.

Sandhill 1894

Sandhill is situated at the foot of Side. The name literally describes the hill of sand that existed here where the Lort (sometimes called Lork, or Loot) Burn flowed into the Tyne. This is the oldest part of Newcastle and was once a bustling commercial centre through which all traffic arriving over the early Tyne bridges passed. The Guildhall, which was built, rebuilt and altered between 1629 and 1823, stands on Sandhill. Opposite is the 17th century house from which Bessie Surtees eloped in 1772 with John Scott (who was later to become Baron Eldon and Lord Chancellor of England). In this photograph, taken in 1894, the Guildhall is out of the picture, to the left of the photographer. The ground floor of Bessie Surtees' House is occupied by 'J.W. Newton'.

The Close c1898

The Close runs parallel to the river, west from Sandhill to Forth Banks. The name refers to the narrowness, or closeness of the street. From medieval days it was the dwelling place of merchants, and by the 17th century many prominent citizens such as Sir John Marley and Sir William Blackett made their homes there. In 1691 the Mansion House was built in The Close for the Mayor of Newcastle. Gradually, as the centre of the town moved up the hill away from the riverside, The Close fell into disrepair. The Mansion House became a timber warehouse and was destroyed by fire in 1895.

Today the area is being restored as part of the Quayside Regeneration Scheme and is the site of attractive public houses and offices.

This photograph from around 1898 shows the narrowness of the street, and its run down appearance at that time.

Akenside Hill c1884

All Saints Church is connected to Side by Akenside Hill. It was originally called All Hallow Bank because of its proximity to the church. Later it became known as Butcher Bank for it was here that many of the town's master butchers lived while they plied their trade in the nearby Flesh Market.

In the late 18th century it was renamed Akenside Hill in honour of the physician and poet Mark Akenside who was born here in 1721. This was also deemed a more suitable name by the middle-class folk who now occupied the street. Akenside's birthplace no longer survives.

Dog Bank c1890

Dog Bank once connected Pilgrim Street with
Akenside Hill and from there the Sandhill. The use
of the word 'dog' in conjunction with a street
name may have a connection with the phrase 'dog-
leg' meaning a sharp bend or narrow passage. As
can be seen from this photograph Dog Bank is
very narrow, and by the 1890s was very run down.
Akenside Hill may be seen at the far end.

Castle Garth 1894

The word 'garth' comes from the old Norse 'garthr', related to the Old English 'geard' or yard. The Castle Yard or Garth contained the Great Hall of the Castle and the old Moot Hall both of which were pulled down in 1809 to make way for the new Moot Hall.

The Castle and its precincts were the property of the Crown and outside the Borough's jurisdiction, although Elizabeth I empowered the town authorities to arrest criminals who had taken refuge in the Castle Garth. In 1812 when the new Moot Hall opened, Newcastle Corporation bought the Castle from the Crown for 600 guineas. The Moot Hall was and still is the province of Northumberland. Originally traders not allowed to trade in the town sold their wares in Castle Garth, a practice eventually prohibited by the Crown, although as late as the turn of the century there were still many cobblers and tailors trading in the narrow streets (now all gone) of Castle Garth.

DOG LEAP STAIRS.

A BIT OF OLD NEWCATLE. 24. Auty.

Dog Leap Stairs 1967

These stairs, seen from the top in the previous photograph of Castle Garth, are situated just above the middle of Side and joined the eastern postern of the Castle to the site of Dean Street. Dog-Lope or Dog-Loup refers to a narrow slip of ground between houses. Dean Street can be seen at the bottom of the stairs.

Javel Groupe c1930

This intriguing name is also closely associated with the Castle. Gavell referred to the King's gaol in the Castle, while a Group was a stream or channel intended to carry the overflow from the moat. Javel Groupe was an alley which ran from The Close, opposite the foot of Long Stairs, to the river. Accounts of the Sheriff of Northumberland in 1356 record that timber for repairs to the Castle was loaded at Javel Groupe. The photograph shows the entrance to No. 4 Javel Groupe.

Side c1855

Often referred to as The Side, this street forms the steep route by the side of the Castle and was originally one of the main passages through the town. At the head of Side, on the site of Milburn House, stood the house where Admiral Collingwood was born on 26th September 1748. Amen Corner can be seen on the left of this photograph, beneath the washing. On the right is a pant—a public fountain.

High Bridge 1969

The High or Upper Dean Bridge spanned the Lort Burn in its deep dene, whose course is indicated today by the line of Grey Street and Dean Street; it flowed into the Tyne at Sandhill. The Burn became a receptacle for butcher's offal and other waste from the nearby Flesh Market. It had steep dangerous banks which presented a problem for traffic between central areas of the town and was eventually covered in. The valley of the Lort Burn can still be seen at the junction of Mosley Street and Dean Street. Here over 30 feet of fill was necessary, and during the redevelopment of the city centre in the 1830s 250,000 cartloads of waste were dumped in the Burn during site levelling.

The name High Bridge has been retained for the street that connects Pilgrim Street to Bigg Market. On the left of this view is the Duke of Wellington public house, famous for its connection with the 6 foot 4 inch, 52 stone Scottish giant William Campbell. When he died in the building, an upper window had to be enlarged to allow the coffin to pass in and out.

Low Bridge 1971

The Low or Nether Dean Bridge linked Pilgrim Street to St Nicholas' Churchyard. It was removed in 1787 when the Lort Burn, which it spanned, was covered over and Dean Street was built. Bourne, in his 18th century history of the Town reports that boats came under the bridge to unload wares. This view shows the site of Low Bridge, off Dean Street near the entrance to the multi-storey car park. The steps lead up to the Tyne Bridge.

Amen Corner 1850 and 1939

Situated behind St Nicholas' Cathedral and connected by stairs to Dean Street, the name as it suggests is associated with the church. The clergy used to hold a procession around the exterior of the Cathedral praying as they went. Amen Corner is where they came to the end of the prayer.

Here was the site of the workshops of some of Newcastle's most famous craftspeople—William and Mary Beilby, glass engravers and Thomas Bewick the wood engraver (remembered in the name of nearby Bewick Street). Joseph Barber the bookseller started Newcastle's first circulating library in 1746 from his house in Amen Corner.

Bigg Market 1928

Bigg is the name of a particular type of barley. Grey's *Chorographia* of 1649 records that 'the Bigg and Oate market is held every Tuesday and Saturday.' The area continued to develop as a commercial centre where a wide range of goods from livestock to crockery could be purchased. The market was held on both sides of the street until the 1920s when the tram route was laid; since then it has been restricted to the north side of the Bigg Market. Carriers left from inns such as the Half Moon in the Bigg Market for destinations including London, Edinburgh, Carlisle and Leeds. Originally the Bigg Market extended into the present Newgate Street until Grainger Street was developed in the 1860s.

The Town Hall, seen in the centre of this photograph, was built in 1858 on the site of Middle Street, but proved unpopular because it obscured the view of St Nicholas' Cathedral.

Groat Market 1827

Opposite the Cathedral is the entrance to the Groat Market. By 1743 this market had been established for the sale of groats (oats from which the hulls have been removed). R.J. Charleton succinctly describes it as 'a street of taverns, tea-rooms and eating houses with some commodious shops on the Town Hall side' (*Newcastle Town*, 1885).

The Groat Market was the most westerly of three streets between Pudding Chare and St Nicholas' Church (it became a Cathedral in 1882) which led to the Bigg Market. Charles Avison, the organist, gave musical evenings in the Assembly Rooms which were situated in the Groat Market. The building was destroyed by fire in 1848.

The Town Post House was in the Groat Market at the junction with Pudding Chare. Just below this was the building known as 'Hell's Kitchen'. Situated in a yard, the kitchen itself was the haunt of beggars, tramps and loafers, while opposite the kitchen were meeting rooms for more respectable citizens. The houses on the left in this picture were demolished in 1838 and the site used to build a Corn Exchange. This in its turn was demolished to make way for a new Town Hall and Corn Exchange in 1858.

Pudding Chare 1897

This photograph shows Pudding Chare where it joins Bigg Market, though the Town Post House has gone. The derivation of the name is not certain, but it could come from the nearby hidden stream, High or Pow Dene, or perhaps from the local delicacy Black Pudding which was sold in the nearby market. Heslop's *Glossary* associates the name with the intestine-like quality of this narrow winding lane which connects Bigg Market with Westgate Road.

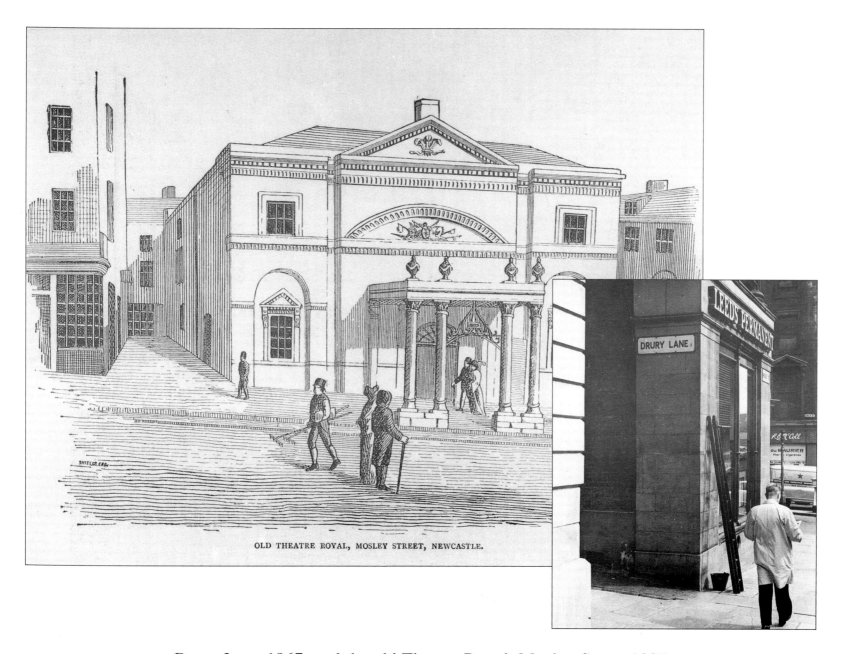

OLD THEATRE ROYAL, MOSLEY STREET, NEWCASTLE.

Drury Lane 1967, and the old Theatre Royal, Mosley Street 1827

Near to the junction of Mosley Street and Grey Street there is a narrow lane leading via a sharp bend to the Cloth Market. In this lane, named after the famous London theatrical street, were entrances to the original Theatre Royal built in 1788. It was demolished by Richard Grainger in the 1830s, along with the Flesh Market, to make way for Grey Street. There was great opposition to his scheme, but Grainger overcame it by promising to build a new theatre and new markets.

Grainger Street c1900

This street was named after Richard Grainger (1797-1861) who, along with architect John Dobson and Town Clerk John Clayton, was responsible for most of the redevelopment of Newcastle town centre during the 1830s. At this time many of the medieval streets and buildings of the town were removed and replaced with the architectural elegance of the 'Tyneside Classical' period.

Originally Grainger Street connected the site of Grey's Monument to the Bigg Market. The link with Neville Street was a narrow, dirty place known as St John's Lane or Copper Alley which was developed in 1868 to become Grainger Street West leading to the Central Station.

Nun Street c1910

When Richard Grainger wanted to replace the old markets demolished to make way for Grey Street, he used a plot of land which had once belonged to a nearby convent, indicated on the map by the area named 'The Nuns'. The Benedictine Nunnery dedicated to St Bartholomew was the first convent to be established in Newcastle. It occupied the area now covered by the Grainger Market and the surrounding land. An entrance to the Nunnery was situated where Nun's Lane meets Nun Street.

Clayton Street c1915

Clayton Street was also formed as part of the redevelopment of the town centre. Opened in 1841, it was named for John Clayton of Chesters, the Town Clerk (1792-1890), who gave his support and financial assistance to the improvements (helping to raise the £2000,000 needed for the whole scheme). Richard Grainger lived in Clayton Street West.

This photograph shows the Picture House cinema on the corner of Clayton Street and Westgate Road. It eventually became the Majestic Ballroom and is now a bingo club.

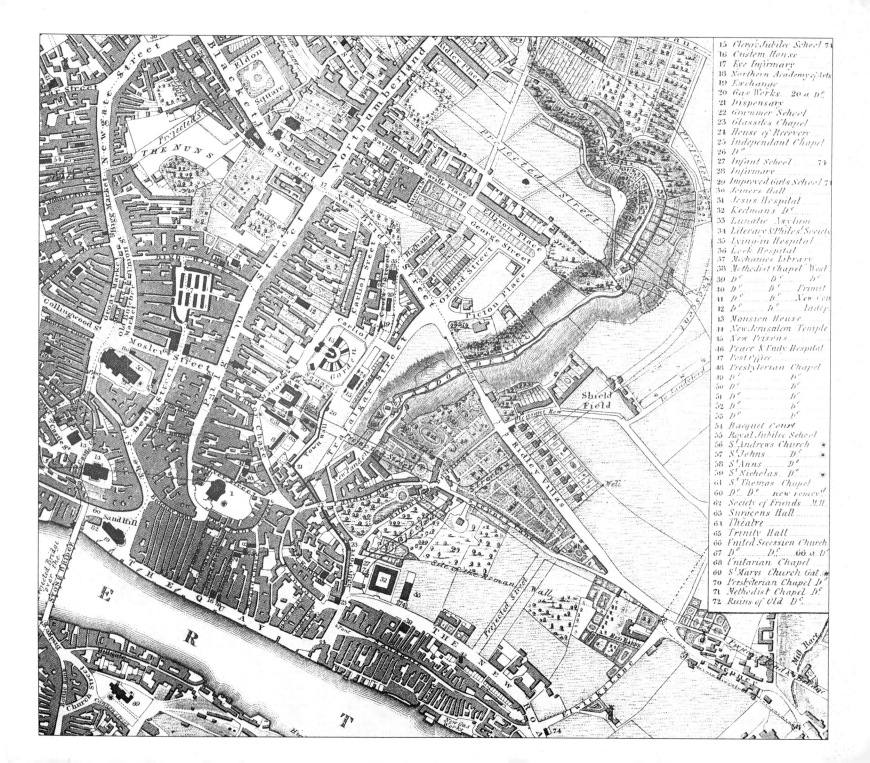

15 *Clergy Jubilee School* 7
16 *Custom House*
17 *Exe Infirmary*
18 *Northern Academy of Arts*
19 *Exchange*
20 *Gas Works.* 20 a D°
21 *Dispensary*
22 *Grammer School*
23 *Glassites Chapel*
24 *House of Recovery*
25 *Independant Chapel*
26 D°
27 *Infant School* 7
28 *Infirmary*
29 *Improved Girls School* 7
30 *Joiners Hall*
31 *Jesus Hospital*
32 *Keelmans* D°
33 *Lunatic Asylum*
34 *Literary & Philos! Society*
35 *Lying-in Hospital*
36 *Leek Hospital*
37 *Mechanics Library*
38 *Methodist Chapel West*
39 D° D° D°
40 D° D° *Primit*
41 D° D° *New Con*
42 D° D° *Indep*
43 *Mansion House*
44 *New Jerusalem Temple*
45 *New Prisons*
46 *Peace & Unity Hospital*
47 *Post Office*
48 *Presbyterian Chapel*
49 D° D°
50 D° D°
51 D° D°
52 D° D°
53 D° D°
54 *Racquet Court*
55 *Royal Jubilee School*
56 *S! Andrews Church*
57 *S! Johns* D°
58 *S! Anns* D°
59 *S! Nicholas* D°
61 *S! Thomas Chapel*
60 D° D° *now remov'd*
62 *Society of Friends* M.H.
63 *Surgeons Hall*
64 *Theatre*
65 *Trinity Hall*
66 *United Secession Church*
67 D° D° 66 a D°
68 *Unitarian Chapel*
69 *S! Marys Church Gat*
70 *Presbyterian Chapel* D°
71 *Methodist Chapel* D°
72 *Ruins of Old* D°

City Road 1879/80

New Road, leading from Milk Market to North Shields, was built in 1776. It was later improved and extended towards Newcastle town centre and in 1882, when Newcastle attained city status, it was renamed City Road.
The Keelmen's Hospital, on the right of the photograph, was built in 1701, financed by the keelmen themselves. Originally it had sixty rooms as well as offices and a club room. Today, after restoration and conversion, it is used for student accomodation.

The Swirle, c1910

The little street known as the Swirle, which runs from St Mary's Street to the Quayside, marks the site of the Swirle Burn which once formed the eastern boundary of the borough of Sandgate. Charleton tells us that the Swirle was sometimes known as the Squirrel and that at one time it was a tidal stream, arched over when the new Quayside was formed early in the nineteenth century.

VIEW IN PANDON DEAN.

New Bridge Street (Pandon Dene 1821)

Pilgrim Street Gate was pulled down at the beginning of the nineteenth century and the stretch of wall from there to Carliol Tower was removed in 1810-12 when New Bridge Street was built. It led to a new bridge across the Pandon Dene, one of the deep denes that cut through the city. At that time Pandon Dene was still a 'sylvan retreat for strolling lovers', and according to Henry Bourne writing in 1736, 'a very romantic place full of hills and vales' (*The History of Newcastle upon Tyne*). Two mills used the Pandon Burn's water for power. When the dene was filled in in the 1880s, the 'new bridge' was demolished. The face of New Bridge Street was radically changed in 1907 when the new Goods Station was built on the edge of Pandon Dene by the North Eastern Railway Company. This building, severely damaged by a bomb on 1 September 1941, was the New Bridge Street Goods Station often wrongly referred to as Manors Goods Station, which was a different building.

Croft Street 1972

The Carliol family, rich thirteenth century merchants, gave their name to the Carliol Tower. The old Central Library on New Bridge Street was built on the site of the Tower in 1880, now marked by the junction of John Dobson Street and New Bridge Street. Inside the eastern wall of the town, south of the tower ran the Carliol Croft, a long garden or orchard. Bourne, writing of the 1730s, describes the walk along the wall overlooking Carliol Croft as 'generally frequented on a Summer's evening by the Gentry of this Part of the Town'. Carliol House today stands across the site of the croft commemorated in Croft Street. This photograph shows Plummer Tower at the bottom of the street.

Carliol Square pre 1924

The Carliols are also commemorated in Carliol Square where between the 1820s and 1924 stood Newcastle's Town Gaol, designed by John Dobson and according to Richardson's *Companion through Newcastle and Gateshead*, 1838, was 'admirably well adapted to the improved system of prison discipline recommended by the philanthropic Howard'. It included a tread mill for the benefit of the prisoners. The prison was demolished to make way for the Telephone Exchange.

Higham Place 1966

One of Richard Grainger's first commissions was to build houses here for Alderman William Batson who lived at Higham Dykes, near Ponteland. Only two of the original houses remain. The building with the tower on the right of this photograph is the Laing Art Gallery opened in 1904. It was presented to the City by Mr Andrew Laing, a wealthy wine merchant. At the foot of Higham Place, on New Bridge Street, is the Lying-in-Hospital designed by John Dobson and opened in 1826. In 1923 the hospital moved to Jubilee Road and the BBC moved into this building, using it as a studio until 1987 when they moved to the 'Pink Palace' in Fenham.

Pilgrim Street 1920

In 1292 Brinkburn Priory was granted land in this street, then called Vicus Peregrinorum. The street is commonly believed to be the route of pilgrims travelling to the shrine of Our Lady of Jesmond, although this explanation of the street name is questioned by some local historians. The Pilgrim Street Gate and Tower separated Pilgrim Street from Northumberland Street. This view shows the southern section of the street, which, at one time, used to slope steeply down towards the Tyne, much as Dean Street does.

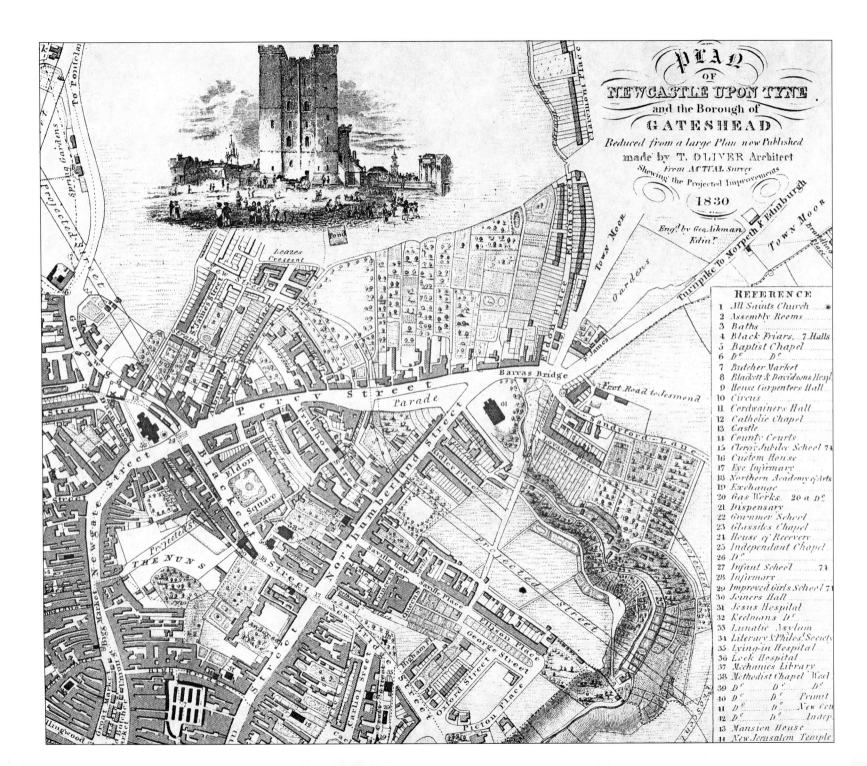

PLAN OF NEWCASTLE UPON TYNE and the Borough of GATESHEAD

Reduced from a large Plan now Published made by T. OLIVER Architect Shewing the Projected Improvements

1830

Engd by Geo. Aikman Edinr

REFERENCE

1. All Saints Church
2. Assembly Rooms
3. Baths
4. Black Friars, 7 Halls
5. Baptist Chapel
6. Do   Do
7. Butcher Market
8. Blackett & Davidsons Hosp.
9. House Carpenters Hall
10. Circus
11. Cordwainers Hall
12. Catholic Chapel
13. Castle
14. County Courts
15. Clergy Jubilee School 7½
16. Custom House
17. Eye Infirmary
18. Northern Academy of Arts
19. Exchange
20. Gas Works   20 a Do
21. Dispensary
22. Grammar School
23. Glassites Chapel
24. House of Recovery
25. Independant Chapel
26. Do
27. Infant School   7½
28. Infirmary
29. Improved Girls School 7½
30. Joiners Hall
31. Jesus Hospital
32. Keelmans Do
33. Lunatic Asylum
34. Literary & Philos! Society
35. Lying-in Hospital
36. Leek Hospital
37. Mechanics Library
38. Methodist Chapel West.
39. Do   Do   Do
40. Do   Do   Primt
41. Do   Do   New Con
42. Do   Do   Indep.
43. Mansion House
44. New Jerusalem Temple

Haymarket / Barras Bridge c1890

The word 'Barras' derives fom the barrows or burial mounds that used to be here, probably linked to the nearby site of the leper hospital. The Bridge in the name refers to the bridge that once carried the road north at this point over the now covered in Pandon Burn.

The piece of land known as Haymarket was a dirty, unseemly waste until 1808 when it was paved and became known as Parade Ground because it was used for inspections of the Newcastle Volunteers. It was renamed Haymarket in 1824 when Newcastle Corporation designated it as the area to be used for the sale of hay. It also continued to be used for diverse purposes such as open-air meetings, wild-beast shows and hirings for agricultural servants. It was closed as a hay market in the 1930s.

St Thomas's Church, on the right of the photograph, was built in 1830 to a design by John Dobson. It stands on the site of the 12th century leper hospital of St Mary Magdalene which in 1660 united with St Thomas's Chapel on the Quayside. When the Chapel was demolished in 1830, it was rebuilt on this site. The Grand Hotel can be seen on the left of this photograph.

Leazes Park c1900

'Leazes' were green pastures reserved for hay-cropping until Lammas at the beginning of August. The word 'Leazes' originally meant to glean or to gather. The Castle Leazes was a gift from King John to the Mayor and Burgesses of Newcastle, and confirmed to them in the reign of Edward III. Covering 127 acres, it was one of three areas of common pasture outside the Town Walls; the others were the Town Moor and Nuns Moor.

Leazes Park, opened in 1873, was the first public park in the town. It covered ten acres: five of water and five of borders and walks. The £2,700 it cost was taken from the Borough Fund used for improvements to the town and for the benefit of inhabitants. Later improvements were financed by income from events such as fireworks and skating on the lake. It cost 6d to skate during the day and 3d after 5.00pm when torchlight was used to illuminate the lake.

Percy Street post 1895

Percy Street was originally known as Sidgate (the street leading towards Side) but was renamed to honour the Percy family. The Norman family of Percy lived in Yorkshire before buying Alnwick Castle in 1309 and settling in Northumberland. They became a prominent family in the region, Harry Percy finding lasting fame as the rebellious Harry Hotspur of Shakespeare's *Henry IV Part 1*. In 1766 the title Earl Percy and Duke of Northumberland was created for the Percy family and continues to be used today.

The early eighteenth century houses in this photograph, reputedly the birth-place of the Newcastle mathematician Charles Hutton, were situated at the corner of Gallowgate and survived until the 1960s. Prior to 1895 Leazes Park Road was known as Albion Road as shown on the map.

Blackett Street c1955

From early times there had been a lane running from Pilgrim Street to New Gate along the line of the Town Wall, but it was not until the improvements to the street, completed in in 1824, that the thoroughfare became an elegant one. The street was named after John Erasmus Blackett (1728-1814), a member of the prominent Newcastle family, and four times Mayor of Newcastle during the eighteenth century. The houses on the left of this photograph date from the 1820s. They were demolished for the Eldon Square shopping centre.

Hunter's Road 1895

Hunter's Road is in Spital Tongues, an area of pasture land once belonging to the hospital of St Mary Magdalene, the leper hospital situated in Barras Bridge.
'Spital' is a common abbreviation for the word hospital, while 'Tongues' refers to the strips of grazing land.
William Hunter was Lord Mayor of Newcastle in 1866. He rented Moor Lodge which was later used as a home for incurables. Eventually a purpose-built hospital was erected in the garden of Moor Lodge, which in the 1930s became known as the St Mary Magdalene Home. In 1948 it was taken over by the Health Service who renamed it Hunter's Moor Hospital. The Hospital is situated behind the wall on the left of this photograph. On the right is the former site of the Spital Tongues Colliery Yard.

Grandstand
Town Moor 1895

Grandstand Road 1895

Grandstand Road is named after the race-course grandstand which was situated on the Town Moor at the site adjacent to the corner of the present Kenton Road. The race course was formed by the Corporation in 1756. The two-storey grandstand, described in Eneas MacKenzie's history of Newcastle as 'an elegant stone edifice' (1827), had galleries which gave a fine view of the entire course. Race meetings were transferred to Gosforth Park in 1882, when the Grandstand was sold. After extensive alteration it became in succession the Bishop Chadwick Memorial Industrial School for Boys, the Grandstand Roller Skating Rink, Armstrong-Whitworth's Aviation Dept. (building fighter planes for World War 1), Lawson's Chocolate Factory and finally Robinson's (later Minories) Garage.

Sandyford Road c1855

Sandyford Road, formerly Sandyford Lane, ran east from Barras Bridge to the present junction with Portland Road and Portland Terrace, a spot previously known as 'Lambert's Leap', where there was a bridge over Sandyford Dene. Sykes, in *Local Records* for September 20 1759, tells us that: 'Mr. Cuthbert Lambert ... was riding along Sandyford-stone Lane, his mare took fright, and, running to the bridge, made a spring over the battlement, which was three and a half feet high, to the opposite side of the burn below, which was 45 feet, and was 36 feet perpendicular.' He escaped with his life, though not by catching hold of a branch as popular legend has it.

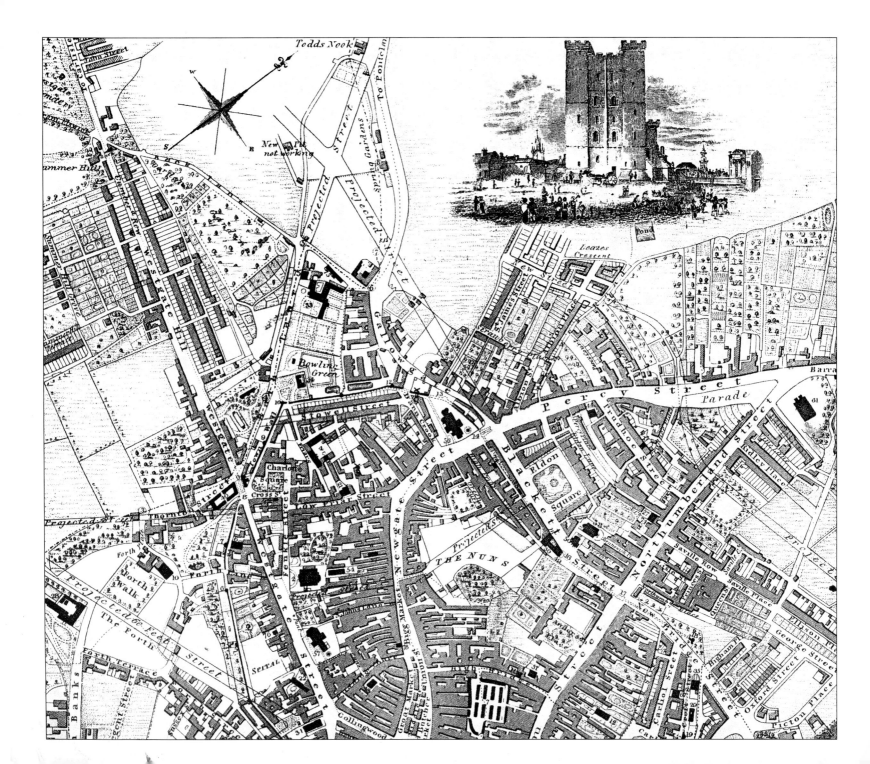

Forth Banks 1900

The Forth was an area of common pasture covering about eleven acres outside the Town Wall. Situated at the westward end of Forth Lane at the top of Forth Banks, the site was later occupied by the Forth Goods Station.

The name probably derives from the old English 'frith' or 'firth'—a space between trees or a shady place. Bourne describes it in the 18th century as 'a mighty pretty place' and 'much frequented by the town's people for its pleasing walk and rural entertainment.' It was square in shape and included a bowling green and a tavern. In 1839 it was the site of Chartist meetings.

In 1752 a General Infirmary was established by subscription on Forth Banks and remained until the Royal Victoria Infirmary was opened in 1906.

Robert and George Stephenson's locomotive works (1824-1900) and Hawthorn's engineering works (later Hawthorn-Leslie) were both situated on Forth Banks. In this 1900 view the site of the railway works can be seen on the left and the goods station on the right.

Bath Lane 1897

The Public Medical Baths were opened here on the west side of the road near Westgate in 1781 by Dr Hall and Messrs H. Gibson and R.B. Abbs, surgeons. The building had an impressive exterior and included a large swimming bath and a 'Buxton' vapour bath. Thomas Oliver's 1831 *Picture of Newcastle upon Tyne* describes it as possessing 'vapour and shower baths, and baths with water either in a hot, cold or tepid state, besides a large open swimming bason'. It was set in attractive gardens, as can be seen from the map.

Low Friar Street 1885

Stretching from Newgate Street to Fenkle Street, Low Friar Street is a reminder that the Dominican Black Friars once occupied land in this area. Their monastery was founded in the 13th century but suffered in the Dissolution of the Monasteries in 1539. This street was once known as Shod Friar Lane after the Dominican friars who wore shoes, unlike the barefoot Greyfriars who occupied land between High Friar Lane and Shakespeare Street.

In 1544 Newcastle Corporation bought the Monastery and it was used to house local craft guilds such as the Smiths and the Cordwainers. It later fell into disrepair but has since been restored to reveal the original cloister pattern of an open space surrounded by walkways.

The photograph shows the 'Dolphin House' (from the carved decoration), since demolished, which was traditionally said to be the oldest house in Newcastle, or the house of the Prior of the Black Friars Monastery, but its history is not known.

Fenkle Street 1897/8

This street is believed to be named after Nicholas Fenkell a merchant who lived in Newcastle in 1577, but the name Fenkle, or derivations from it, is in use throughout Northern England.

The building on the left in this photograph is Cross House, originally the site of the home of Ralph Carr who founded the first bank in Newcastle. Cross House was damaged by fire in 1912.

Bull Park, mentioned on the banner displayed on Cross House was the original name for the Exhibition Park, the site where the town bull grazed. The park was renamed in 1887 to celebrate Queen Victoria's Jubilee but the new name was not commonly used until 1929.

Pink Lane 1884/1886

The Pink Tower stood at the junction of Pink Lane and Clayton Street West; it was demolished in 1852 to make way for John Knox Chapel and its loss was regretted by some. A Mr Fenwick writing in 1861 concerning the demolition of the nearby Gunner Tower described the Pink Tower as 'a characteristic and picturesque object'. Perhaps this might be a reference to the hue of the building and a possible explanation of the origin of the name 'Pink' which our researches have been unable to discover. Pink Lane follows the line of the 'Pomerium', a narrow alley which gave access to the nearby Town Wall. Adjoining the building on the south side of Pink Lane are the foundations of Gunner Tower.

Newgate Street 1910

The New Gate, which gave its name to the street, was one of the six gates in the Town Wall in existence in the 14th century and in his 1827 history of Newcastle, Mackenzie suggests that it stood on the site of an earlier gate called Berwick Gate. New Gate gatehouse was used as the Town Gaol until 1828, when a new Town Gaol was opened in Carliol Croft. Newgate Street was part of the thoroughfare leading from the Side, across Bigg Market, curving past St Andrew's Church to the New Gate. This photograph shows the site of the Green Market on Newgate Street, by St Andrew's Churchyard.

Gallowgate, looking West, 1894

Gallowgate led from the New Gate Gaol to the town gallows, outside the Town Wall near the site of St James' Park. Brand describes them as being 'on the entrance to the Town Moor'. Prisoners from the town were executed here while those from the county were executed outside the West Gate at a site near the present Tyne Theatre. The last person to be hanged on the Town Moor was Mark Sherwood of Blandford Street, in 1844, for the murder of his wife. Bourne's *History of Newcastle upon Tyne*, 1736, describes Gallowgate as 'a very tolerable street, and a very pleasant Place having in it some good Houses which are situated in Gardens and Fields'.

Darn Crook 1899

The origin of the name Darn Crook is doubtful. Darn may be derived from 'dark', while Crook may refer to the bent or crooked nature of the lane now called St Andrew's Street (though locals still call it Darn Crook). Until 1810, when a way was cut through, the street was a cul-de-sac with the Town Wall at the north end. It was here in 1644 that the Scottish General Baillie and his troops breached the Town Wall during the Civil War.
In this view St Andrew's Churchyard is on the right, while on the left is the present site of the Newcastle Co-operative Society Store. In 1899 the tannery in Darn Crook was owned by J. G. Fenwick & Co.